Magnificent Maths

Shaun Stirling

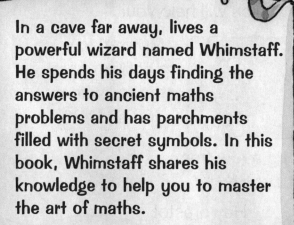

In a cave far away, lives a powerful wizard named Whimstaff. He spends his days finding the answers to ancient maths problems and has parchments filled with secret symbols. In this book, Whimstaff shares his knowledge to help you to master the art of maths.

Whimstaff has a goblin assistant named Pointy, who is very clever. Pointy helps Whimstaff perfect his spells and gets annoyed with the laziness of Mugly and Bugly, his fat pet frogs. They spend most of their time eating and sleeping and do as little work as possible.

Pointy also helps Whimstaff look after Miss Snufflebeam. She is a young dragon who is rather clumsy and often loses Whimstaff's numbers!

Wizard Whimstaff and his friends are very happy solving maths problems. Join them on a magical quest to win the Trophy of Maths Wizardry!

Contents

Awesome Ordering

I'm Wizard Whimstaff!
Before you can use maths magic you must be able to put numbers in order. Look at this pattern taken from my magical number grid which will help you:

110	111	<u>112</u>
210	211	<u>212</u>
31<u>0</u>	31<u>1</u>	<u>312</u>

Moving down a column from top to bottom you add 100.

Moving along a row from left to right you add 1.

Hey presto!

Task 1   Use your magic to fill in the missing numbers.

a   109   110   ▯   ▯   113   114

b   546   547   548   ▯   ▯   552

c   ▯   249   ▯   ▯   253   254   255

d   993   ▯   ▯   997   998   999

Task 2   Arrange these numbers on the row from smallest to largest. Abracadabra!

348   351   346   347   352   349   350   345

▯ ▯ ▯ ▯ ▯ ▯ ▯ ▯

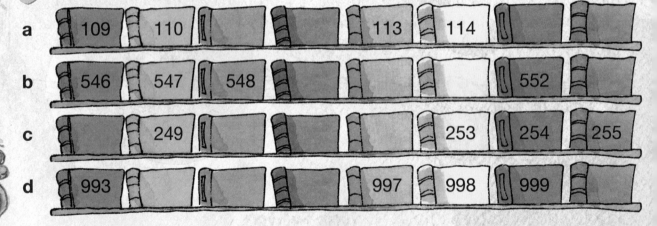

Task 3

Now use your new ordering skills to fill in the gaps. Don't worry if it seems hard at first. Look at Wizard Whimstaff's pattern for help.

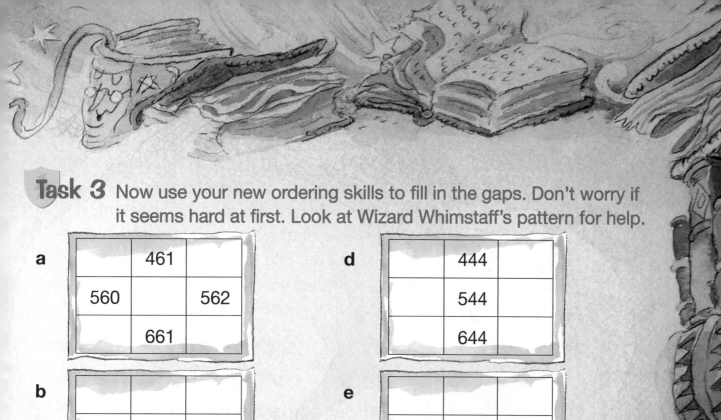

a

	461	
560		562
	661	

d

	444	
	544	
	644	

b

204		206
	305	

e

		300
	399	

c

	599	
698		700

f

	549	

Sorcerer's Skill Check

Allakazan! Clumsy Miss Snufflebeam has made a hole in my number grid. Can you repair it by putting in the missing numbers?

406	407	408	409	410	411
506	507			510	511
606					611
706					711
806	807			810	811
906	907	908	909	910	911

Super work! Add your first silver shield to your trophy on page 32.

Playful Partitions

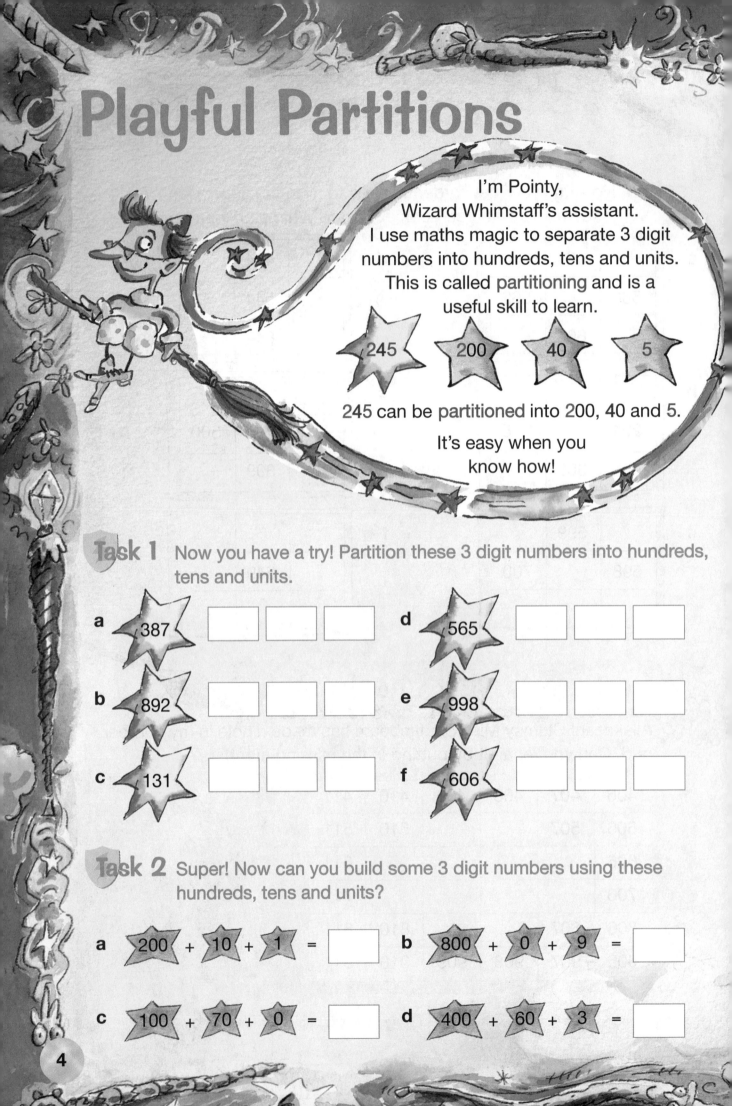

I'm Pointy,
Wizard Whimstaff's assistant.
I use maths magic to separate 3 digit
numbers into hundreds, tens and units.
This is called partitioning and is a
useful skill to learn.

245   200   40   5

245 can be partitioned into 200, 40 and 5.

It's easy when you
know how!

Task 1   Now you have a try! Partition these 3 digit numbers into hundreds,
tens and units.

a   387

d   565

b   892

e   998

c   131

f   606

Task 2   Super! Now can you build some 3 digit numbers using these
hundreds, tens and units?

a   200 + 10 + 1 =

b   800 + 0 + 9 =

c   100 + 70 + 0 =

d   400 + 60 + 3 =

4

Task 3 Now write the number that is written in words in each star. Then put them together to build some more 3 digit numbers. Practice makes perfect!

a one hundred + eighty + two =

b six hundred + ten + three =

c two hundred + seventy + six =

d seven hundred + eighty + zero =

Sorcerer's Skill Check

One more task! These hundreds, tens and units stars are all muddled up. Colour the stars to show which 3 digit number they come from. You'll soon get the hang of it!

115 **952** **468** **634**

a 600

b 900

c 100

d 400

e 30

f 50

g 10

h 60

i 4

j 2

k 5

l 8

Croak! Give yourself another silver shield, smarty pants.

Amazing Adding

Wizards like me use three magic pointers to make addition easier.

⭐ Know your **number bonds!**

$0 + 6$ $1 + 5$

6

$2 + 4$ $3 + 3$

⭐ If you are adding three numbers look for **number pairs** that make 10, then add the numbers that are left.

6 **3** **4**

$6 + 4 = 10$
$10 + 3 = 13$

⭐ Use a **number line.**

15 16 17 18 19 20 21 22 23 24 25

$16 + 7 = 23$

Task 1 Wave your wand and work out the answer for each sum. Then colour it so it is the same colour as these totals.

10 = pink   12 = green   14 = blue

a $2 + 12 =$ _____

e $3 + 7 =$ _____

g $6 + 6 =$ _____

c $5 + 7 =$ _____

f $5 + 9 =$ _____

b $4 + 8 =$ _____

d $4 + 6 =$ _____

h $4 + 10 =$ _____

Task 2 Hey presto! These numbers are muddled up, but you will find the totals quite easily if you look for pairs that make 10 first.

a 7 5 3 ☐

b 5 8 5 ☐

c 1 9 9 ☐

d 8 2 4 ☐

e 4 3 6 ☐

f 8 7 3 ☐

Task 3
Abracadabra! My magic number line will help you find the answers to these sums. Remember to start with the largest number.

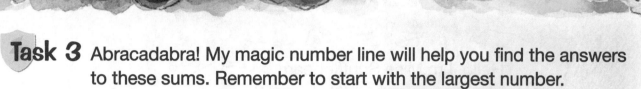

a 11 + 7 = ☐   **b** 15 + 5 = ☐   **c** 16 + 1 = ☐

d 13 + 4 = ☐   **e** 14 + 4 = ☐   **f** 6 + 13 = ☐

Task 4
Did the magic work? Try these too. They're a bit harder.

a 18 + 9 = ☐   **b** 4 + 22 = ☐   **c** 17 + 9 = ☐

d 3 + 19 = ☐   **e** 20 + 5 = ☐   **f** 7 + 17 = ☐

Sorcerer's Skill Check

Use your magic one more time to fill in these addition squares.

a

+	12	2	7
13			
10		12	
8			

b

+	14	17	4
10			
6			
13			

c

+		16	9
10	25		
14			
	26		20

d

+	4		9
22		27	
3		8	
	16		

That seemed very hard to me! Give yourself a silver shield.

Charming Charts

Hello, I'm Miss Snufflebeam and I get very confused by charts!

Bar charts allow you to see and compare different types of data. Look at this chart showing some of my pets.

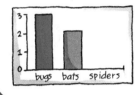

I can see that I have more bugs than bats, and no spiders.

Task 1 Wizard Whimstaff wants me to create a spell. He has left me this bar chart which shows how much of each ingredient I need. Help me by answering these questions.

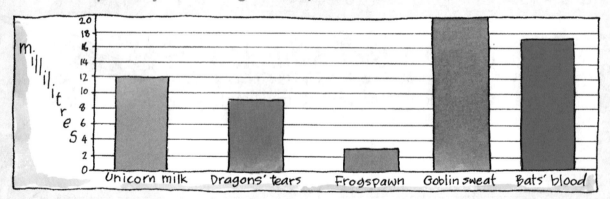

a How many millilitres of unicorn milk do I need? _____ml

b How many millilitres of dragons' tears do I need? _____ml

c How many more millilitres of goblin sweat than bats' blood do I need? _____ml

d How many millilitres of frogspawn and dragons' tears do I need altogether? _____ml

e Which ingredient do I need the most of? _____

f Which ingredient do I need the least of? _____

8

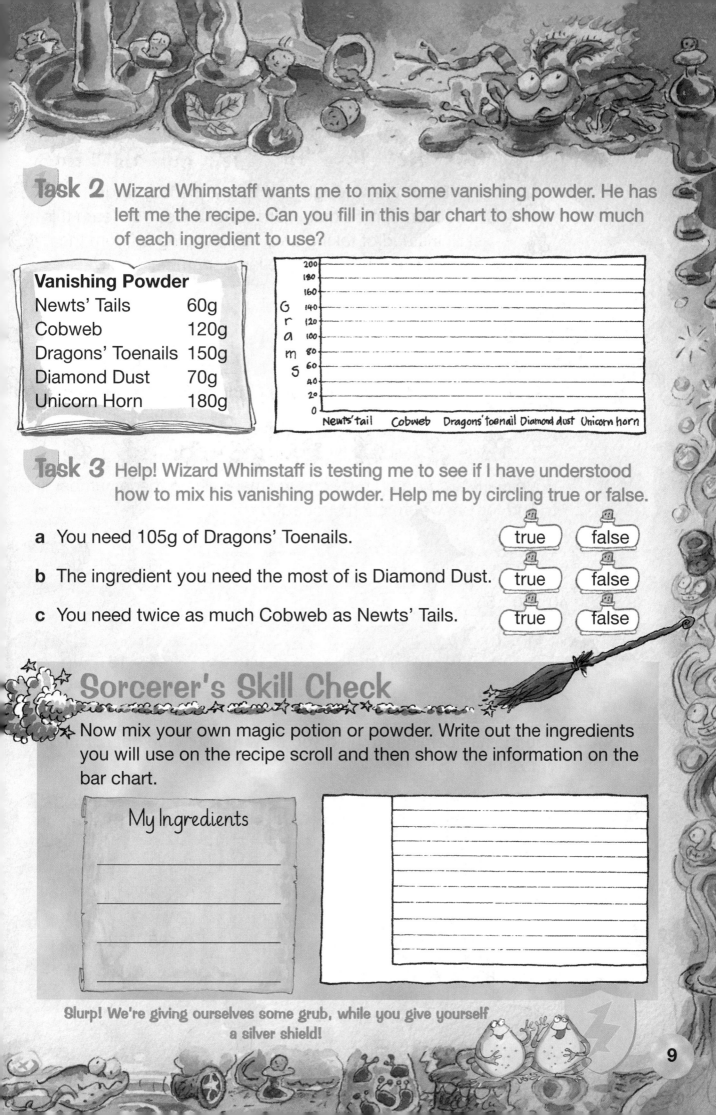

Task 2 Wizard Whimstaff wants me to mix some vanishing powder. He has left me the recipe. Can you fill in this bar chart to show how much of each ingredient to use?

Vanishing Powder

Newts' Tails	60g
Cobweb	120g
Dragons' Toenails	150g
Diamond Dust	70g
Unicorn Horn	180g

Grams:
200
180
160
140
120
100
80
60
40
20
0

Newts' tail · Cobweb · Dragons' toenail · Diamond dust · Unicorn horn

Task 3 Help! Wizard Whimstaff is testing me to see if I have understood how to mix his vanishing powder. Help me by circling true or false.

a You need 105g of Dragons' Toenails. true false

b The ingredient you need the most of is Diamond Dust. true false

c You need twice as much Cobweb as Newts' Tails. true false

Sorcerer's Skill Check

Now mix your own magic potion or powder. Write out the ingredients you will use on the recipe scroll and then show the information on the bar chart.

My Ingredients

_____

_____

_____

Slurp! We're giving ourselves some grub, while you give yourself a silver shield!

Scary Subtraction

Burp! We're Mugly and Bugly, the lazy frogs! Subtraction can be quite hard work unless you learn this skill. Instead of taking away, try hopping up from the smaller number to the larger number. Look.

$84 - 47 = ?$

47 50 80 84

Now add up the hops you made to find the answer:

$3 + 30 + 4 = 37$

Task 1 Brain cell alert! Add up the hops we made along these number lines to find the answer to each subtraction.

a

+2 +10 +6

38 40 50 56

☐ + ☐ + ☐ = ☐ $56 - 38 =$ ☐

b

+4 +20 +4

16 20 40 44

☐ + ☐ + ☐ = ☐ $44 - 16 =$ ☐

Task 2 Use the number lines to help you draw in your own hops. Hurry, grub's up!

a

13 20 30 31

☐ + ☐ + ☐ = ☐ $31 - 13 =$ ☐

b

29 30 80 85

☐ + ☐ + ☐ = ☐ $85 - 29 =$ ☐

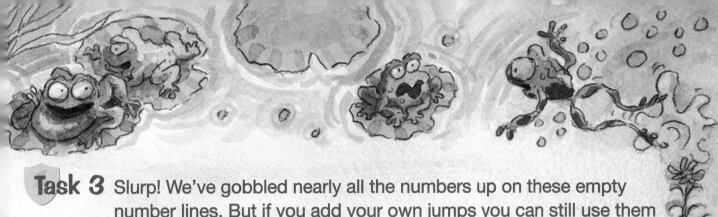

Task 3

Slurp! We've gobbled nearly all the numbers up on these empty number lines. But if you add your own jumps you can still use them to work out each subtraction.

a

29 [ ] [ ] 66

[ ] + [ ] + [ ] = [ ]

66 – 29 = [ ]

b

16 [ ] [ ] 43

[ ] + [ ] + [ ] = [ ]

43 – 16 = [ ]

c

17 [ ] [ ] 83

[ ] + [ ] + [ ] = [ ]

83 – 17 = [ ]

Sorcerer's Skill Check

Cross our pond by hopping between lily pads. Write the new number you make on each pad. When you arrive at the other side, colour in the toad with the correct total.

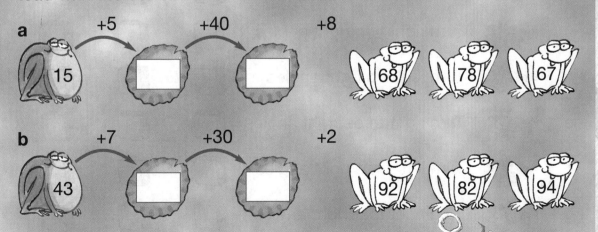

a 15 +5 → [ ] +40 → [ ] +8   68 78 67

b 43 +7 → [ ] +30 → [ ] +2   92 82 94

Rabracadada! Give yourself a silver shield for counting on so well!

Alarming Angles

Oh dear! When Wizard Whimstaff sends me on errands I often get lost. He says I must learn **left** and **right**, and that a **quarter turn** is called a **right angle**. This is the plan he has done to show me how:

Forward 3.
Turn right one right angle.
Forward 2.

Task 1 Oops! I've forgotten left and right. Help me to remember by completing this task. Tick the direction I should be pointing in after I make each of these turns.

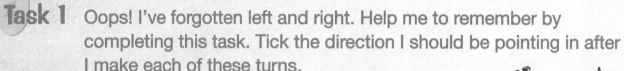

starting position					
a	Turn left one right angle	☐	☐	☐	☐
b	Turn right one right angle	☐	☐	☐	☐
c	Turn right two right angles	☐	☐	☐	☐
d	Turn left two right angles	☐	☐	☐	☐
e	Turn right three right angles	☐	☐	☐	☐
f	Turn left three right angles	☐	☐	☐	☐
g	Turn right four right angles	☐	☐	☐	☐
h	Turn left four right angles	☐	☐	☐	☐

Task 2 Help! I have to run four errands for Wizard Whimstaff. He's given me these instructions to follow. Can you tell me where I'll end up if I start each errand from the same place?

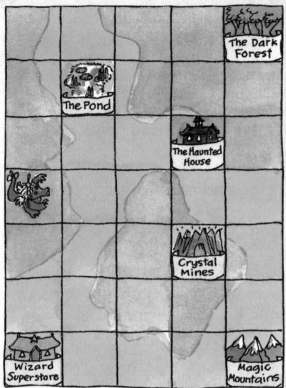

a Turn right one right angle.
Forward 3.

_____

b Forward 4. Turn right one right angle. Forward 3.

_____

c Turn left one right angle. Forward 2. Turn right one right angle. Forward 1.

_____

d Turn right one right angle. Forward 1. Turn left one right angle. Forward 3.

_____

Sorcerer's Skill Check

Oh no! I've wandered into a magic mist whilst out for a stroll! Can you give instructions that tell me how to get safely to one side without going through the mist?

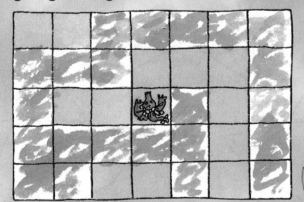

_____

_____

_____

_____

_____

Well done, young apprentice! Add another well-earned shield
to your trophy.

Apprentice Wizard Challenge 1

Challenge 1 Fill in the gaps in these number lines.

a 596 597 598 [ ] [ ] [ ] 602 603

b 205 [ ] 207 [ ] 209 [ ] 211 [ ]

c [ ] 101 [ ] 103 [ ] 105 [ ] 107

Challenge 2 Partition these 3 digit numbers onto these hundreds, tens and units stars.

Hundreds   Tens   Units   Hundreds   Tens   Units

a 514 = ☆ + ☆ + ☆   b 108 = ☆ + ☆ + ☆

c 987 = ☆ + ☆ + ☆   d 222 = ☆ + ☆ + ☆

Challenge 3 Complete these addition stars by adding all five points. Write the total in the centre of the star.

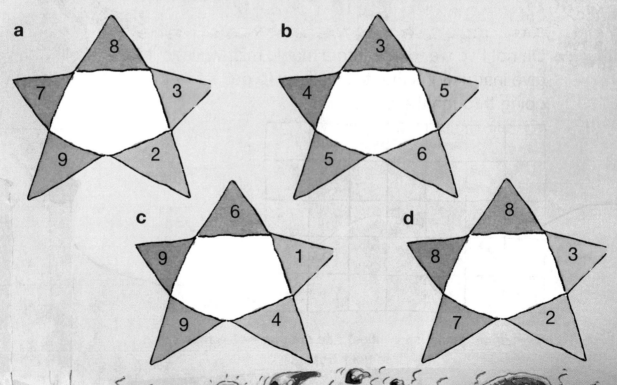

a   8   7   3   9   2

b   3   4   5   5   6

c   6   9   1   9   4

d   8   8   3   7   2

Challenge 4

Pointy has cleared these creatures out of the cave. Show how many of each animal he has found by drawing bars onto this chart.

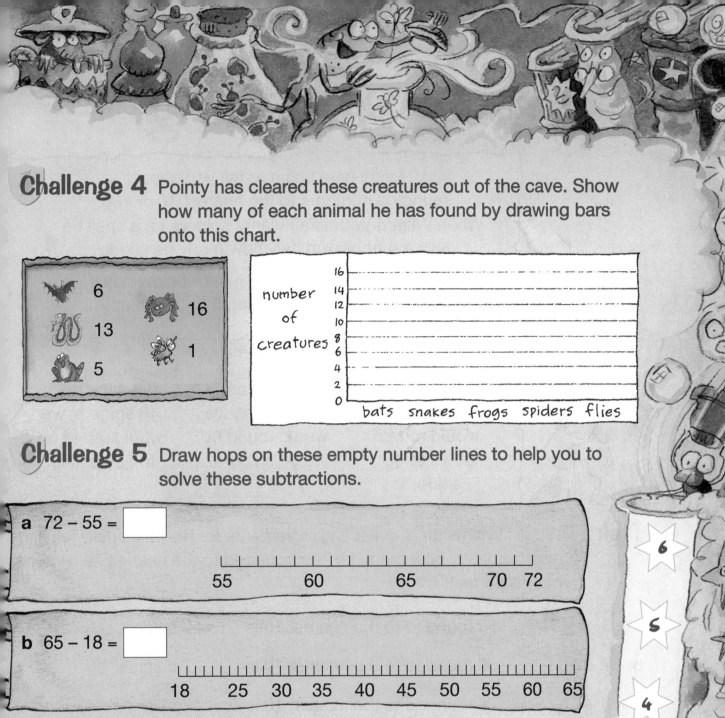

Challenge 5

Draw hops on these empty number lines to help you to solve these subtractions.

a 72 – 55 = ☐

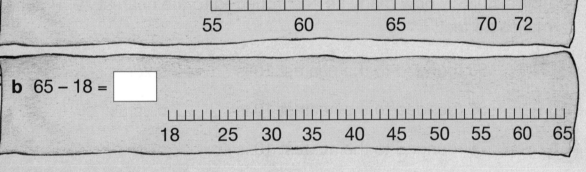

```
55          60          65          70  72
```

b 65 – 18 = ☐

```
18      25    30    35    40    45    50    55    60    65
```

Challenge 6

Trace these instructions with a pen and reveal the number that Wizard Whimstaff is making.

Forward 2
Turn left one right angle   Forward 2
Turn left one right angle   Forward 2
Turn right one right angle   Forward 2
Turn right one right angle   Forward 2

Count how many challenges you got right and put a star on the test tube to show your score. Then have another silver shield for your trophy!

Challenge Score

6
5
4
3
2
1

Revolting Rounding

Pointy here again to tell you about rounding numbers to the nearest 10 or 100. When Wizard Whimstaff wants spiders for a spell he tells me **approximately** how many he needs.

We round numbers ending in 4 or below down. We round numbers ending 5 or above up.

40 41 42 43 44 45 46 47 48 49 50

If there are 43 spiders, we would round down to 40 spiders.

If there are 45 spiders, we would round up to 50 spiders.

If there are 48 spiders, we would round up to 50 spiders.

Task 1

Wizard Whimstaff is collecting ingredients for his next spell. Tell him approximately how many he has, rounded to the nearest 10. Practice makes perfect!

a 53   53 rounded to the nearest 10 is _____ spiders

b 67   67 rounded to the nearest 10 is _____ crystals

c 78   78 rounded to the nearest 10 is _____ owls

Task 2

Wizard Whimstaff is mixing some powerful magic. Super! This time he wants his ingredients rounded to the nearest 100. I've done the first o for you, can you do the rest?

380   400   420   440   460   480   500   520

a *10 Quality Dragon Puffs 420g*   420g rounded to the nearest 100g is _400_ g

b *Bottled Pixie Laughter 515g*   515g rounded to the nearest 100g is _____ g

c *Goblin Beards 480g*   480g rounded to the nearest 100g is _____ g

d *Stardust 450g*   450g rounded to the nearest 100g is _____ g

Task 3 Use a ruler to measure the length of these magic wands. Write their length to the nearest centimetre. Remember to always round up if you measure half way between one centimetre and the next. I've done the first one for you!

a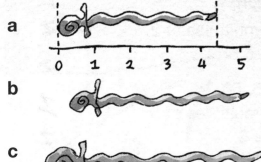

This wand is __4__ cm long, rounded to the nearest centimetre

b

This wand is _____ cm long, rounded to the nearest centimetre

c

This wand is _____ cm long, rounded to the nearest centimetre

d

This wand is _____ cm long, rounded to the nearest centimetre

e

This wand is _____ cm long, rounded to the nearest centimetre

Sorcerer's Skill Check

Round the numbers to the nearest 10 and then colour them to match the code. It's easy when you know how!

Nearest 40	Pink
Nearest 50	Yellow
Nearest 60	Blue
Nearest 70	Green

74 48 42

45 65

44 63 56

What a well rounded education you are receiving! Give yourself another silver shield.

Mysterious Multiples

We need to learn the 2, 5 and 10 times tables, but it sounds too much like hard work! Luckily we know a rule about the numbers in each table that should make it easy.

2, 4, 6, 8, 10, 12, 14, 16, 18, 20
Numbers in the 2 times table are called multiples of 2.
They always end in either 0, 2, 4, 6 or 8.

5, 10, 15, 20, 25, 30, 35, 40, 45, 50
Numbers in the 5 times table are called multiples of 5.
They always end in either 0 or 5.

10, 20, 30, 40, 50, 60, 70, 80, 90, 100
Numbers in the 10 times table are called multiples of 10.
They always end in 0.

Task 1 Grubs up! These cauldrons are cooking up the 2, 5 and 10 times tables. Draw a ring around the multiples that belong to each cauldron.

a
2× table
14   30   45
19   57   76
98   63

b
5× table
100   64   5
51   75   45
86   97

c
10× table
123   10   45
250   101   76
110   300

Task 2 Croak! Use what you know about multiples of 2, 5 and 10 to help you continue these patterns.

a   (226)   (228)   (230)   (   )   (   )   (   )

b   (100)   (105)   (110)   (   )   (   )   (   )

c   (770)   (780)   (790)   (   )   (   )   (   )

Task 3 In this 100 square, colour all the multiples of 2 yellow. Draw a circle around all the multiples of 5. Draw a triangle around all the multiples of 10. Talk about the patterns that you notice, but not to us!

1	2	3	4	5	6	7	8	9	10
11	12	13	14	15	16	17	18	19	20
21	22	23	24	25	26	27	28	29	30
31	32	33	34	35	36	37	38	39	40
41	42	43	44	45	46	47	48	49	50
51	52	53	54	55	56	57	58	59	60
61	62	63	64	65	66	67	68	69	70
71	72	73	74	75	76	77	78	79	80
81	82	83	84	85	86	87	88	89	90
91	92	93	94	95	96	97	98	99	100

Sorcerer's Skill Check

Before we have a snooze, look at this special table called a Venn Diagram. Can you sort the numbers on our list into the correct spaces on the diagram. Sounds like a job for Pointy!

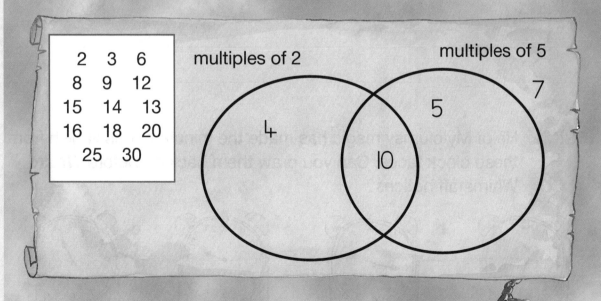

2	3	6
8	9	12
15	14	13
16	18	20
	25	30

multiples of 2

multiples of 5

4

5

7

10

You soon got the hang of multiples! Have another shield!

Tremendous Time

Oh dear! I'm late for an errand! If only I was better at reading the time! I know these:

o'clock	half past	quarter to	quarter past

It's the ones in between I get wrong. Pointy has drawn me this clock to help me remember minutes past and minutes to.

Task 1 Dabracababra! What time is it on each of these clocks?

a

b

c

d

_____ _____ _____ _____

e

f

g

h

_____ _____ _____ _____

Task 2 Help! My clumsy magic has made the minute hands vanish from these clock faces. Can you draw them back on before Wizard Whimstaff notices?

a

10 minutes
past 5

b

20 minutes
to 9

c

25 minutes
past 2

d

5 minutes
to 1

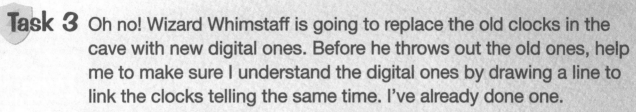

Task 3 Oh no! Wizard Whimstaff is going to replace the old clocks in the cave with new digital ones. Before he throws out the old ones, help me to make sure I understand the digital ones by drawing a line to link the clocks telling the same time. I've already done one.

Sorcerer's Skill Check

I think I understand now. Before we go, colour in the time on these digital clocks to show me how you spend your day!

a Wake up

b Eat my lunch

c Eat my tea

d Start school

e Finish school

f Bedtime!

You're a clever timekeeper! Magic another shield onto your trophy.

Magical Money

When we go shopping, Mugly always writes an amount in pence.

 This can of slime costs 170p.

Bugly always writes an amount in pounds and pence.

These cans of spiders cost £1.70.

Luckily, we're both right, as long as we don't use the pounds and pence signs together. Burp!

Task 1 Complete these price tags so that we can both read them.

a
£2.50   p

b

50p   £

c

185p
£

Task 2 Slurp! Pointy has given us some money to go shopping. Total up the coins and write the amount in pence and then pounds. We're off for a snooze. All this counting is making us tired!

a   = [   ] p = £[   ]

b   = [   ] p = £[   ]

c   = [   ] p = £[   ]

d   = [   ] p = £[   ]

Task 3 This time Pointy has sent us shopping with a £2 coin. Write in the missing coins that the shopkeeper gave us and the total change we would receive, while we have a snooze!

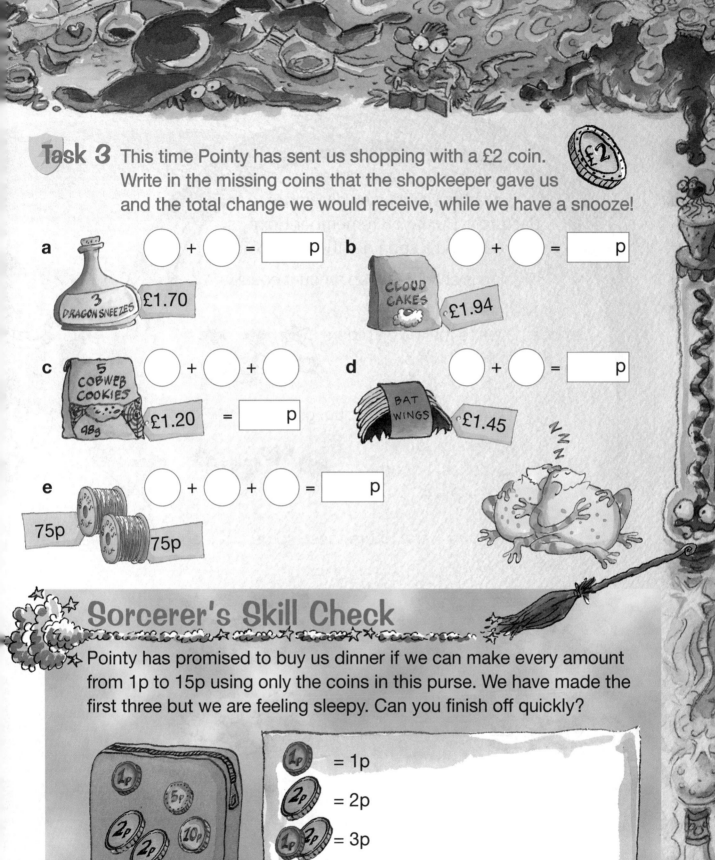

a ◯ + ◯ = ☐ p

3 DRAGON SNEEZES £1.70

b ◯ + ◯ = ☐ p

CLOUD CAKES £1.94

c ◯ + ◯ + ◯

5 COBWEB COOKIES 98g £1.20 = ☐ p

d ◯ + ◯ = ☐ p

BAT WINGS £1.45

e ◯ + ◯ + ◯ = ☐ p

75p 75p

Sorcerer's Skill Check

Pointy has promised to buy us dinner if we can make every amount from 1p to 15p using only the coins in this purse. We have made the first three but we are feeling sleepy. Can you finish off quickly?

1p = 1p

2p = 2p

1p 2p = 3p

Allakazan! You're a whizz with money! Award yourself another silver shield.

Dazzling Division

Lots of apprentice maths wizards say division is dastardly. But if you remember Pointy's pointers you'll soon get the hang of it.

⭐ Division is sharing out an amount equally.

6 spiders shared equally between 3 webs makes 2 spiders fror each web.

$6 \div 3 = 2$

⭐ Division is making equal groups.

8 spiders grouped into 2s makes 4 groups.

$8 \div 2 = 4$

Task 1 Now you have a try! Share these spiders out equally between the webs.

a $9 \div 3 = \boxed{}$

b $12 \div 4 = \boxed{}$

c $15 \div 3 = \boxed{}$

d $12 \div 2 = \boxed{}$

Task 2 Super! Now draw circles around the bats below to split them into equal groups, and count the number of groups you make.

a $10 \div 2 = \boxed{}$

b $14 \div 7 = \boxed{}$

c $12 \div 3 = \boxed{}$

d $16 \div 4 = \boxed{}$

Task 3 How many different ways can you find to divide these bats into equal groups? Write a division sentence for each way. It's easy when you know how!

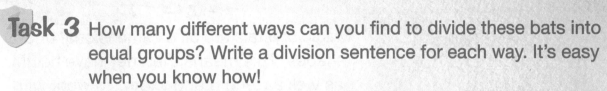

a 18 ÷ ☐ = ☐   **b** 18 ÷ ☐ = ☐   **c** 18 ÷ ☐ = ☐

d 18 ÷ ☐ = ☐   **e** 18 ÷ ☐ = ☐   **f** 18 ÷ ☐ = ☐

Sorcerer's Skill Check

Nearly done! Work out the division sum on each web. Then draw a line to the correct spider so they know which webs are theirs.

2

3

4

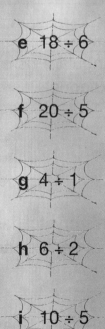

a 14 ÷ 7

b 15 ÷ 5

c 12 ÷ 3

d 20 ÷ 10

e 18 ÷ 6

f 20 ÷ 5

g 4 ÷ 1

h 6 ÷ 2

i 10 ÷ 5

My head hurts just watching you work! You deserve another silver shield!

Spellbinding Shapes

Magic crystals are all 3-Dimensional or 3-D shapes. This means that they have height as well as length and width. To work with 3-D shapes you need to be able to use the correct words to describe their properties.

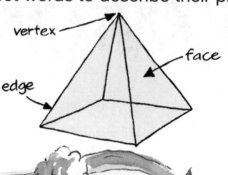

vertex

face

edge

Task 1 Abracadabra! Complete this table of information about the crystals that I use. I have done the first one for you.

Crystal	Number of		
	Vertices	Edges	Faces
Pyramid	5	8	5
Cube			
Cuboid			
Triangular Prism			
Hexagonal Prism			

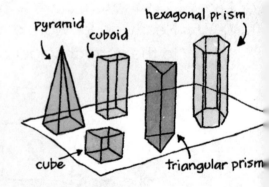

pyramid   cuboid   hexagonal prism

cube   triangular prism

Task 2 Now have a go at this exercise. Which crystal am I describing? Use the table and the pictures to help.

a This crystal has 2 triangular faces that are the same shape and size.

_____

b This crystal has 6 faces and they are all the same shape.

_____

c This crystal has 1 square face and 4 triangular faces.

_____

d This crystal has twice as many vertices as the triangular prism.

_____

Task 3 Prisms are special kinds of crystals. Each prism has a particular 2-Dimensional or 2-D shape that you see when you cut across its length. Draw lines to match the prism to the shape I get when I cut it.

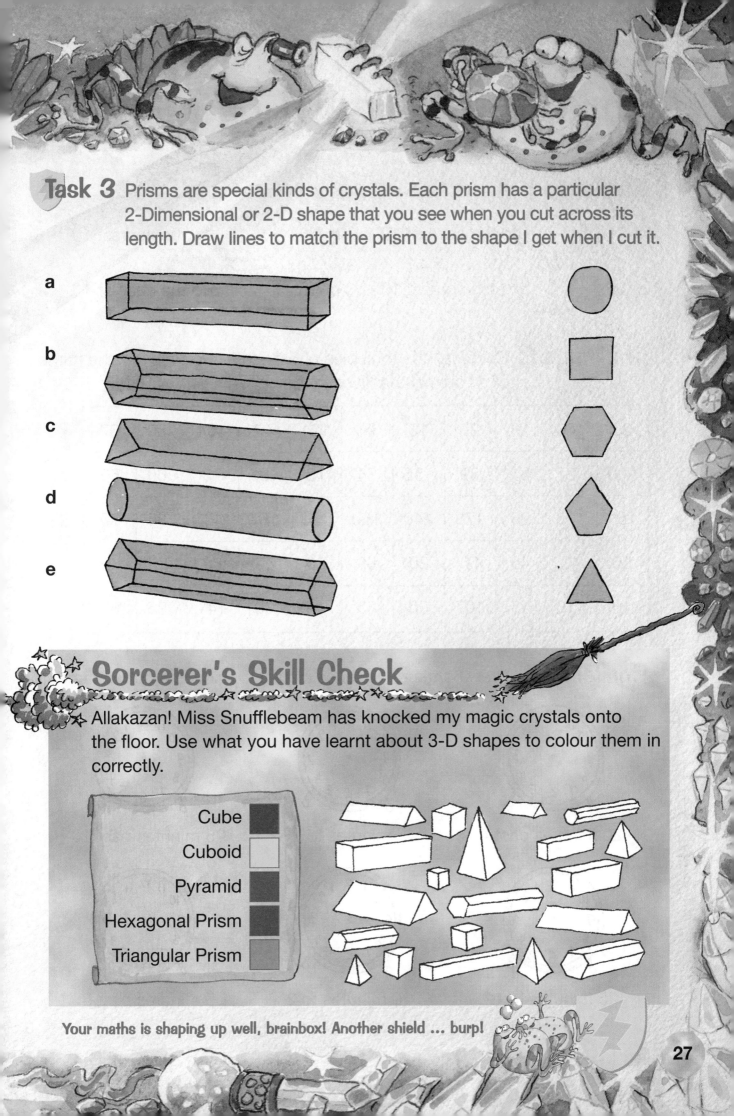

a

b

c

d

e

Sorcerer's Skill Check

Allakazan! Miss Snufflebeam has knocked my magic crystals onto the floor. Use what you have learnt about 3-D shapes to colour them in correctly.

Cube

Cuboid

Pyramid

Hexagonal Prism

Triangular Prism

Your maths is shaping up well, brainbox! Another shield ... burp!

Apprentice Wizard Challenge 2

Challenge 1   Round these numbers to the nearest 10.

a 77 _____ to the nearest 10   **b** 35 _____ to the nearest 10

c 96 _____ to the nearest 10   **d** 15 _____ to the nearest 10

Challenge 2   Colour all the multiples of 5 on this grid to reveal the name of an animal that lives in the cave.

25	103	16	27	13	91	121	42	104	80	57
100	2	51	89	156	34	73	191	75	60	50
5	125	25	178	140	150	120	167	11	35	76
55	43	40	56	20	66	30	42	88	115	134
10	110	15	107	90	85	45	70	141	95	65

Challenge 3   Draw hands on to these clocks to show the correct time.

a

20 minutes past 4

b

5 minutes to 7

c

25 minutes past 10

d

25 minutes to 12

e

10 minutes to 2

f

5 minutes past 5

Challenge 4 Total up these coins and write the amount in pounds and pence.

a  50p 50p 50p 20p 5p 5p 2p = [ ] p = £ [ ]

b £2 20p 20p 20p 10p 1p = [ ] p = £ [ ]

c £1 £1 £1 £1 £1 5p 1p 1p = [ ] p = £ [ ]

d 20p 20p 20p 20p 20p 10p 5p = [ ] p = £ [ ]

Challenge 5 Fill in the gaps in these division sentences.

a $5 \div 1 = $ [ ]

b $15 \div 3 = $ [ ]

c $12 \div 4 = $ [ ]

d $20 \div$ [ ] $= 10$

e $9 \div$ [ ] $= 3$

f $18 \div 2 = $ [ ]

g [ ] $\div 3 = 4$

h $16 \div 4 = $ [ ]

Challenge 6 Use the clues to sort out what these jumbled up 3-D shapes are.

a If you cut me across my length you get a hexagon.

alphemiragsonx _____

b I have one square face and four triangular faces.

mydripa _____

c I have six square faces.

becu _____

d I have 8 vertices but I am not a cube.

bidocu _____

6

5

4

3

2

1

Challenge Score

Count how many challenges you got right and put stars on the test tube to show your score. Then take the last silver shield for your trophy!

Answers

Pages 2–3

Task 1 **a** 111, 112, 115, 116
  b 549, 550, 551, 553
  c 248, 250, 251, 252
  d 994, 995, 996, 1000

Task 2 345, 346, 347, 348, 349, 350,
  351, 352

Task 3 **a** 460 461 462   **d** 443 444 445
    560 561 562   543 544 545
    660 661 662   643 644 645
  b 104 105 106   **e** 198 199 200
    204 205 206   298 299 **300**
    304 305 306   398 399 400
  c 598 599 600   **f** 448 449 450
    698 699 700   548 549 550
    798 799 800   648 649 650

Sorcerer's Skill Check
  406 407 408 409 410 411
  506 507 508 509 510 511
  606 607 608 609 610 611
  706 707 708 709 710 711
  806 807 808 809 810 811
  906 907 908 909 910 911

Pages 4–5

Task 1 **a** 300, 80, 7
  b 800, 90, 2
  c 100, 30, 1
  d 500, 60, 5
  e 900, 90, 8
  f 600, 0, 6

Task 2 **a** 211   **b** 809
  c 170   **d** 463

Task 3 **a** 100 + 80 + 2 = 182
  b 600 + 10 + 3 = 613
  c 200 + 70 + 6 = 276
  d 700 + 80 + 0 = 780

Sorcerer's Skill Check
  blue: c, g, k
  red: b, f, j
  orange: d, h, l
  green: a, e, i

Pages 6–7

Task 1 **pink:** e, d
  green: b, c, g
  blue: a, f, h

Task 2 **a** 15   **d** 14
  b 18   **e** 13
  c 19   **f** 18

Task 3 **a** 18   **d** 17
  b 20   **e** 18
  c 17   **f** 19

Task 4 **a** 27   **d** 22
  b 26   **e** 25
  c 26   **f** 24

Sorcerer's Skill Check

a +	12	2	7
13	25	15	20
10	22	12	17
8	20	10	15
b +	14	17	4
10	24	27	14
6	20	23	10
13	27	30	17
c +	15	16	9
10	25	26	19
14	29	30	23
11	26	27	20
d +	4	5	9
22	26	27	31
3	7	8	12
12	16	17	21

Pages 8–9

Task 1 **a** 12ml   **d** 12 ml
  b 9ml   **e** goblin sweat
  c 3ml   **f** frogspawn

Task 2

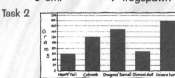

Task 3 **a** false   **b** false
  c true

Sorcerer's Skill Check.
  Check that child's recipe and bar
  chart match.

Pages 10–11

Task 1 Values in additions can appear in
  any order but encourage child to put
  larger values first.
  a 10 + 6 + 2 = 18
  b 4 + 20 + 4 = 28

Task 2 **a** 7, 10, 1
    7 + 10 + 1 = 18
    31 – 13 = 18
  b 1, 50, 5
    1 + 50 + 5 = 56
    85 – 29 = 56

Task 3 **a**
  29   30   60   66
    1 + 30 + 6   = 37
  b
  16   20   40   43
    4 + 20 + 3   = 27
  c
  17   20   80   83
    3 + 60 + 3   = 66

Sorcerer's Skill Check
  a Numbers on lily pads: 20 and 60.
    Toad 68 coloured in.
  b Numbers on lily pads: 50 and 80.
    Toad 82 coloured in.

Pages 12–13

Task 1 **a**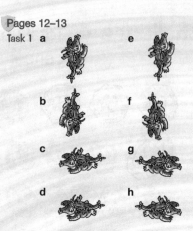

Task 2 a Wizard's Superstore
  b Magic Mountains
  c The Pond
  d Crystal Mines

Sorcerer's Skill Check
  Forward 1. Turn right one right
  angle. Forward 2. Turn right one
  right angle. Forward 3.

Pages 14–15

Challenge 1
  a 599, 600, 601
  b 206, 208, 210, 212
  c 100, 102, 104, 106

Challenge 2
  a 500 + 10 + 4
  b 100 + 0 + 8
  c 900 + 80 + 7
  d 200 + 20 + 2

Challenge 3
  a 29   **b** 23
  c 29   **d** 28

Challenge 4

Challenge 5
  a 17   **b** 47

Challenge 6
  Wizard Whimstaff has traced the
  number 5 in the sky.

Pages 16–17

Task 1 **a** 50 spiders   **b** 70 crystals
  c 80 owls

Task 2 **a** 420g rounded to the nearest
    100g is 400g
  b 515g rounded to the nearest
    100g is 500g
  c 480g rounded to the nearest
    100g is 500g
  d 450g rounded to the nearest
    100g is 500g

Task 3 a This wand is 4cm long, rounded to the nearest centimetre.
b This wand is 5cm long, rounded to the nearest centimetre.
c This wand is 6cm long, rounded to the nearest centimetre.
d This wand is 2cm long, rounded to the nearest centimetre.
e This wand is 5cm long, rounded to the nearest centimetre.

Sorcerer's Skill Check
Spiders are coloured as indicated:
44 & 42 pink; 45 & 48 yellow;
56 & 63 blue; 65 & 74 green.

Pages 18–19
Task 1 a These numbers are ringed:
14; 30; 76; 98
b These numbers are ringed:
100; 5; 75; 45
c These numbers are ringed:
10; 250; 110; 300

Task 2 a 232, 234, 236 **b** 115, 120, 125
c 800, 810, 820

Task 3 The 2s, 4s, 6s, 8s and 10s columns should be coloured yellow. Numbers in the 5s and 10s columns should have circles drawn around them. Numbers in the 10s column should also have triangles drawn around them.

Sorcerer's Skill Check

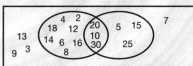

Pages 20–21
Task 1 a 20 minutes past 3
b 5 minutes past 4
c 25 minutes to 8
d 10 minutes past 11
e 5 minutes to 12
f 10 minutes to 6
g 25 minutes past 5
h 20 minutes to 7

Task 2 a **b**

c **d**

Task 3 a 06:35 **d** 12:05
b 08:10 **e** 09:20
c 02:50

Sorcerer's Skill Check
Responses will depend upon the child's own timetable.

Pages 22–23
Task 1 a 250p
b £0.50
c £1.85

Task 2 a 460p = £4.60
b 180p = £1.80
c 506p = £5.06
d 211p = £2.11

Task 3 a 20p + 10p = 30p change
b 5p + 1p = 6p change
c 50p + 20p + 10p = 80p change
d 5p + 50p = 55p change
e 20p + 20p + 10p = 50p

Sorcerer's Skill Check
It is possible to make all totals from 1p to 15p e.g.
2p + 2p = 4p
5p = 5p
5p + 1p = 6p
5p + 2p = 7p
5p + 2p + 1p = 8p
5p + 2p + 2p = 9p
10p = 10p
10p + 1p = 11p
10p + 2p = 12p
10p + 2p + 1p = 13p
10p + 2p + 2p = 14p
10p + 5p = 15p

Pages 24–25
Task 1 a 9 ÷ 3 = 3 **b** 12 ÷ 4 = 3
c 15 ÷ 3 = 5 **d** 12 ÷ 2 = 6

Task 2 a 10 ÷ 2 = 5 **b** 14 ÷ 7 = 2
c 12 ÷ 3 = 4 **d** 16 ÷ 4 = 4

Task 3 There are 6 possible number sentences:
18 ÷ 6 = 3 18 ÷ 3 = 6
18 ÷ 2 = 9 18 ÷ 9 = 2
18 ÷ 18 = 1 18 ÷ 1 = 18

Sorcerer's Skill Check
Linked with a line to spider '2' should be:
14 ÷ 7 = 2; 20 ÷ 10 = 2; 10 ÷ 5 = 2.
Linked with a line to spider '3' should be:
15 ÷ 5 = 3; 6 ÷ 2 = 3; 18 ÷ 6 = 3.
Linked with a line to spider '4' should be:
12 ÷ 3 = 4; 20 ÷ 5 = 4; 4 ÷ 1 = 4.

Pages 26–27
Task 1
Table completed as follows:

Crystal	Number of		
	Vertices	Edges	Faces
Pyramid	5	8	5
Cube	8	12	6
Cuboid	8	12	6
Triangular Prism	6	9	5
Hexagonal Prism	12	18	8

Task 2 a Triangular Prism
b Cube
c Pyramid
d Hexagonal Prism

Task 3 Check that:
a cuboid is linked to rectangle;
b hexagonal prism is linked to hexagon;
c triangular prism is linked to triangle;
d cylinder is linked to circle;
e pentagonal prism is linked to pentagon.

Sorcerer's Skill Check
The child's colouring should have identified 4 of each 3-D shape.

Pages 28–29
Challenge 1
a 80 **b** 40
c 100 **d** 20

Challenge 2
The word 'bat' should be revealed.

Challenge 3
a **d**

b **e**

c **f**

Challenge 4
a 182p = £1.82
b 271p = £2.71
c 507p = £5.07
d 115p = £1.15

Challenge 5
a 5 ÷ 1 = 5
b 15 ÷ 3 = 5
c 12 ÷ 4 = 3
d 20 ÷ 2 = 10
e 9 ÷ 3 = 3
f 18 ÷ 2 = 9
g 12 ÷ 3 = 4
h 16 ÷ 4 = 4

Challenge 6
a hexagonal prism
b pyramid
c cube
d cuboid

The end

Wizard's Trophy of Excellence

Awesome Ordering

Playful Partitions

Revolting Rounding

Mysterious Multiples

Amazing Adding

Charming Charts

Tremendous Time

Magical Money

Scary Subtraction

Alarming Angles

Dazzling Division

Spellbinding Shapes

Apprentice Wizard Challenge 1

Apprentice Wizard Challenge 2

This is to state that Wizard Whimstaff awards

Apprentice _____

the Trophy of Maths Wizardry. Congratulations!

Published 2002

10 9 8 7

Letts Educational, The Chiswick Centre,
414 Chiswick High Road, London W4 5TF
Tel 0845 602 1937   Fax 020 8742 8767
Email mail@lettsed.co.uk
www.Letts-SuccessZone.com

Text, design and illustrations © Letts Educational Ltd 2002

Author: Shaun Stirling
Book Concept and Development:
Helen Jacobs, Publishing Director; Sophie London, Project Editor
Series Editor: Lynn Huggins-Cooper
Design and Editorial: 2idesign ltd, Cambridge
Cover Design: Linda Males
Illustrations: Mike Phillips and Neil Chapman (Beehive Illustration)
Cover Illustration: Neil Chapman

British Library Cataloguing in Publication Data

A CIP record for this book is available from the British Library.

ISBN 978-1-84315-125-8

Printed and bound in Italy

Colour reproduction by PDQ Digital Media Solutions Limited,
Bungay, Suffolk.